OUR DAY OUT

Our Day Out displays all the chaos and hilarity that result when
Mrs Kay's 'Progress Class' are unleashed for a day's coach trip to
Conway Castle in Wales — via the café, the zoo, the beach and the
fun fair. It is an exuberant celebration of the joys and agonies of
growing up and being footloose, fourteen and free from school.
But *Our Day Out* is more than a mere romp — it points up the
depressing present and empty future for these comprehensive
no-hopers, for whom a day out is as much as they can expect.

'The skill and zest of the show . . . derive from its success in
following the adult argument through while preserving all the fun
of a story for and mainly played by children . . . I have rarely
seen a show that combined such warmth and such bleakness.'
Irving Wardle, *Times*

'Fast, funny and curiously moving'   Carol Wilks, *Guardian*

'Fresh, lively and natural'   Stella Flint, *Daily Telegraph*

Adapted from the television play, the script published here,
complete with songs by Willy Russell, Bob Eaton and Chris
Mellors, is Russell's musical version, written for Liverpool's
Everyman Theatre, and staged there and at London's Young Vic
in 1983.

D0401425

OUR DAY OUT

A Play by Willy Russell

with Songs and Music by
Bob Eaton, Chris Mellors
and Willy Russell

A Methuen Paperback

METHUEN YOUNG DRAMA

First published as a Methuen Paperback original in 1984
by Methuen London Ltd, 11 New Fetter Lane, London EC4P 4EE
and Methuen Inc., 29 West 35th Street, New York, NY 10001, USA
Reprinted 1985, 1986, 1987
Our Day Out copyright © 1984 by Willy Russell
Songs and music copyright © 1984
by Bob Eaton, Chris Mellors and Willy Russell
Set in IBM 9 pt Press Roman by 🅰 Tek-Art, Croydon, Surrey
Printed in Great Britain by Richard Clay Ltd, Bungay, Suffolk

British Library Cataloguing in Publication Data
Russell, Willy
    Our day out. – (Methuen young drama)
    I. Title
    822'.914   PR6073.U/

ISBN 0-413-54870-8

Our Day Out was originally written as a television play and transmitted as a BBC 'Play for Today' in 1976. It was subsequently adapted for the stage and first performed on 8 April 1983, with the following cast:

MRS KAY	Linda Beckett
BUS DRIVER/ZOO KEEPER/LES	Carl Chase
COLIN/HEADMASTER	David Hobbs
MR BRIGGS	Robert McIntosh
SUSAN/CAFÉ OWNER	Christina Nagy

The Children

X Company*: Sue Abrahams, Michaela Amoo, Danny Ayers, Maria Barrett, Angela Bell, Andy Broadhead, Maxine Cole, Vernon Eustace, Brian Hanlon, Michael Kagbo, Andrea Langham, Victor McGuire, Mary Shepherd, Paul Spencer, Charlie Thelu, Jason Williams
Y Company*: Hannah Bond, Peter Bullock, Shaun Carr, Mary Farmer, Danny Jones, Anne Lundon, Ritchie Macauley, Keith Maiker, Jacqui McCarthy, Victor McGuire, Jocelyn Meall, Joanne Mogan, Joanne Oldham, Joanne Pennington, Ben Wilson, John Winstanley
    **X and Y performed on alternate nights*

Directed by Bob Eaton and Kate Roland
Musical direction by Chris Mellor
Designed by Sue Mayes
Lighting designed by Kevin Fitzsimons

Our Day Out was subsequently seen at the Young Vic Theatre, London, from 20 August 1983, with the following cast:

MRS KAY	Rosalind Boxall
BUS DRIVER/ZOO KEEPER/LES	Martin Stone
COLIN/HEADMASTER	William Gaminara
MR BRIGGS	Stephen Lewis
SUSAN/CAFÉ OWNER	Christina Nagy

The Children: Matthew Barker, Paul Billings, Gillian Blavo, Maura Hall, Michelle Bristol, Richard Cotterill, Brian Warrington, Tony Fuller, Jane Gibbs, Claire Mitchell, Paul Harbert, Roy Spicer, Sally Hobbs, Tony Jones, Darragh Murray, Darryl Niven, Marie Quetant, Jason Robertson, Jaqueline Rodger, Elizabeth Toone

Directed by Bob Eaton
Musical direction by Stuart Barham
Designed by Sue Mayes
Lighting by Andy Phillips

Author's Note

Language and Setting

For the purpose of publication I have retained the play's original settings of Liverpool and Wales but this is not intended to imply that productions of the play in other parts of the country should strive to observe the original setting or reproduce the idiom in which it is written. If being played in, say, Sheffield, the play would, I feel, be more relevant to both cast and audience if adapted to a local setting and the local accent.

Following the play's original production in Liverpool it was staged at The Young Vic where it became a Cockney play: the setting of the school became Hackney, the Mersey Tunnel became the Blackwall Tunnel, Conway Castle became Bodiam Castle, the Welsh Coast, the South Coast and so on.

I can foresee a problem where the play is set in an area which has no road tunnel or bridge and if this is the case, would suggest that you simply cut this small section of script.

Staging

Although it would be possible to present the play on a proscenium stage I think it's much better suited to a more flexible area. The play was originally presented in the round, with a set that consisted of a number of simple benches. These benches were used as the seats on the coach and then rearranged by the actors to suggest the various other settings – the café, the zoo, even the rocks on the beach.

Two platforms were built at a higher level and were used as the castle battlements, the cliff and the headmaster's study.

In both the Everyman and Young Vic productions the coach carried about fifteen to twenty passengers. Obviously this number could be increased for large-cast productions.

Music

Again, in the original productions of the play, the production budgets demanded that the musical accompaniment be kept to an absolute minimum – i.e., piano and percussion. Should you be in the happy position of knowing no such constraints and have at your disposal a band or orchestra, please feel free to arrange the music accordingly.

Willy Russell

ACT ONE

As we hear the musical introduction for the first song, we see
LES, *the Lollipop man, enter. He is very old, almost blind and can
hardly walk. A group of* KIDS, *on their way to school, enter,
shouting 'Hia Les,' 'All right there Les' and singing:*

KIDS: We're goin' out
Just for the day
Goin' off somewhere far away
Out to the country
Maybe to the sea
Me Mam says I can go . . . if it's free

During verse two the KIDS *exit singing and* CAROL *enters
also singing.*

CAROL:⎫ The sky is blue
KIDS: ⎰ The sun's gonna shine
Better hurry up cos it's nearly nine
This is the day that's
Just for us
We're goin' out . . . on a bus

CAROL *is about to make her way to the school when she
notices* LES *on the other side of the road.*

CAROL: Hia Les.

LES (*trying to see*): Who's that?

CAROL (*crossing to him*): Carol, it's Carol, Les.

LES: Hello love. 'Ey, can y' see me back across the road? (*As
she takes his arm and leads him back.*) You're early today
aren't y'?

CAROL: Yeh. We're goin' out. On a trip.

LES: Where to?

CAROL: I dunno. It's somewhere far away. I forget.

LES: Are they all goin'?

CAROL: Only the kids in the Progress Class.

LES: The what?

CAROL: Don't y' know what the Progress Class is? It's Mrs Kay's
class. Y' go down there in the week if y' can't do readin' or
sums or writin'. If you're backward like.

LES: By Christ, I'll bet she's kept busy. They're all bloody
backward round here.

CAROL: I know. I better be goin' now, Les. I'm gonna be late.
An' there's Briggs!

We see BRIGGS *approaching as* LES *calls to* CAROL.

LES: Tarar girl. Mind how you go.

CAROL (*running off*): See y' Les.

LES (*to* BRIGGS *who is about to cross the road*): 'Ey, you! Don't move.

BRIGGS: I beg your pardon.

LES: Wait. There.

BRIGGS: Look, I've not got the time to . . .

LES: No one crosses the road without the assistance of the Lollipop man, no one.

BRIGGS: Look man . . .

LES: The Government hired me!

BRIGGS: But there's nothing coming.

LES: How do you know? How do you know a truck or a car isn't gonna come speedin' out of one of them side roads? Eh? How can you set an example to kids if you're content to walk under the wheels of a juggernaut?
LES goes to the centre of the road and waves BRIGGS *across.*
That's why the Government hires me!
MRS KAY and KIDS enter.

KIDS (*singing*):
Mrs Kay's Progress Class
We're the ones who
Never pass
We're goin' out
Off with Mrs Kay
We're goin' out . . . today

MRS KAY: All right all right . . . Will you just let me have a bit of peace and I'll get you *all* sorted out. Right, now look (*She spells it out.*) all those . . . who've got permission to come on the trip . . . but who haven't yet paid . . . I want you to come over here.
She separates herself from the group. Every kid follows her.
BRIGGS *passes and surveys the scene with obvious disapproval.*

MRS KAY (*bright*): Morning, Mr Briggs.

BRIGGS (*grudging*): Morning.
He turns towards the school as a couple of KIDS *emerge.*
Come on, you two. Where are you supposed to be? Move!
The BOYS *rush to the safety of* MRS KAY's *group and* BRIGGS *goes off.*

KIDS (*sing as a round*):
> Got a packed lunch
> Got money to spend
> Gonna get a seat near my best friend
> Just can't wait to get
> Away from here
> Gonna bring me Mam . . . a souvenier

As the round ends the KIDS *are blacked out. They rearrange the benches to form the\coach, as we see* BRIGGS *enter the* HEADMASTER's *study.*

BRIGGS: When was this arranged?

HEAD: Don't talk to me about it. After the last trip of hers I said 'no more', absolutely no more. Look, just look. (*He indicates a file.*) Complaints from the residents of Derbyshire.

BRIGGS: Well how the hell's she arranged this then?

HEAD: When I was away at conference. George approved it in my absence. He wasn't aware of any ban on remedial department outings.

BRIGGS: It'll have to be cancelled.

HEAD: If it is she'll resign.

BRIGGS: Good. The school would be better off without her.

HEAD: There's not many of her type about y' know. By and large I reckon she does a good job. She keeps them well out of the way with their reading machines and plasticine. It's just when she gets let loose with them.

BRIGGS: OK. I'll have to go with her, won't I?
Blackout HEAD's *study as we bring up* MRS KAY *talking to a young teacher,* SUSAN. *Around them are lively excited* KIDS *in random groups. Two* KIDS *are pulling and pushing each other.*

MRS KAY: Maurice! Come away from that road!

MAURICE: I'm sorry, miss.

MRS KAY: Come on, keep on the side where it's safe.
Two older KIDS *(fifteen) come rushing out of school and approach the* teachers.

REILLY: Ey, miss hang on, hang on . . . can we come with y', miss. Can we?

DIGGA: Go on, miss, don't be tight, let's come.

REILLY: Go on, miss . . . say yeh.

MRS KAY: Brian, you know it's a trip for the Progress Class.

REILLY: Yeh, well, we used to be in the Progress Class didn't we?

SUSAN: But Brian, you're not in the Progress Class any longer, are you? Now that you can read and write you're back in normal classes.

REILLY: Agh, miss, come on . . .

MRS KAY: Brian, you know that I'd willingly take you, but it's not up to me. Who's your form teacher?

REILLY: Briggsy.

MRS KAY: Well . . . I'll take you, if you get his permission.

REILLY (*as he and* DIGGA *run off*): Ogh . . . you're sound, miss.

MRS KAY: BRIAN!
  He stops.
  Bring a note.

REILLY: Ah miss, what for?

MRS KAY: Because I wasn't born yesterday and if I don't ask you to bring a note you'll hide behind that wall for two minutes and then tell me Mr Briggs gave permission.

REILLY: As if we'd do something like that, miss.

MRS KAY: I want it in writing.

CAROL (*tugging at* MRS KAY*'s arm as* REILLY *and* DIGGA *go off*): Where we goin' eh miss?

MRS KAY: Carol! Miss Duncan's just told you: Conway, we're going to Conway.

CAROL: Is that in England miss?

SUSAN: It's in Wales Carol.

CAROL: Will we have to get a boat?
  COLIN *enters, running.*

COLIN: Sorry I'm late . . . Car wouldn't start.

LINDA: Hia sir.

JACKIE. Hia sir.

COLIN: Hello girls. (*Avoiding them. Or trying to.*) Erm, Mrs Kay . . .

LINDA: Sir, I thought for a minute you weren't comin' on the trip. I was heart broken.

COLIN: Yes erm . . . er . . .

CAROL: Miss, how will we get there?

MRS KAY: Carol! We're going on a coach. Look. There. (*She shouts to all the* KIDS.) You can get on now. Go on . . .

There is a wild rush of KIDS *to the coach but suddenly the* DRIVER *is there, blocking their way.*

DRIVER: Right. Just stop there. No one move!

KID: Miss said we could get on.

DRIVER: Oh did she now?

KIDS: Yeh.

DRIVER. Well let me tell youse lot somethin' now. Miss is not the driver of this bus. I am. An' if I say y' don't get on, y' don't get on.

As we hear the intro for 'Boss of the Bus'.

DRIVER (*sings*):
This is my bus
I'm the boss of the bus
I've been drivin' it for fifteen years
This is my bus
I'm the boss of the bus
So just pin back your ears
I'm the number one
I'm the driver man
And you kids don't get on
Till I say you can

This is my bus
I'm the boss of the bus
And the lesson I want learned
This is my bus
I'm the boss of the bus
And as far as I'm concerned
If you wanna put
One over on me
You're gonna need a damn sight more
Than a GCE

Don't want no lemonade, no sweets
Don't want no chewing gum
Cos the bleedin' stuff gets stuck to the seats
And respectable passengers' bums

This is my bus
I'm the boss of the bus
And I've seen it all before
This is my bus
I'm the boss of the bus
And I don't want no spew on the floor
I don't want no mess

Don't want no fuss
So keep your dirty hands
From off of my bus.
This is my bus

KIDS: He's the boss of the bus

DRIVER: This is my bus

KIDS: He's the boss of the bus

DRIVER: This is my bus

KIDS: He's the boss of the bus

DRIVER: This is my bus

KIDS: He's the boss of the bus
There's nothing wrong with us

DRIVER (*heaving off a* KID *who managed to get onto the bus*):
Get off of my bus.

MRS KAY: Is there something the matter, driver?

DRIVER: Are these children in your charge, madam?

MRS KAY: Yes.

DRIVER: Well you haven't checked them have y'?

MRS KAY: Checked them? Checked them for what?

DRIVER: Chocolate and lemonade! We don't allow it. I've seen
it on other coaches, madam; fifty-two vomitin' kids, it's no
joke. I'm sorry but we don't allow that.

MRS KAY (*to* SUSAN): Here comes Mr Happiness. All right,
driver, I'll check them for you. Now listen, everyone: if
anyone has brought chocolate or lemonade with them I want
them to put up their hands.
A sea of innocent faces and unraised hands.
There you are, driver, all right?

DRIVER: No it's not all right. Y' can't just take their word for it.
They have to be searched. You can't just believe kids.
Pause. She could blow up but she doesn't.

MRS KAY: Can I have a word with you, driver, in private?
The DRIVER *comes off the coach. She manoeuvres it so that
the* DRIVER *has his back to the* KIDS *and other* TEACHERS.
What's your name, driver?

DRIVER: Me name? I don't usually have to give me name.

MRS KAY: Oh come on. What's your name?

DRIVER: Schofield, Ronnie Schofield.

MRS KAY: Well, Ronnie. (*She points.*) Just take a look at those
streets.

*He does so and as he does she motions, behind his back,
indicating that the other* TEACHERS *should get the* KIDS
onto the coach.
Ronnie, would you say they were the sort of streets that
housed prosperous parents?

DRIVER: We usually do the better schools.

MRS KAY: All right, you don't like these kids, I can see that. But
do you really have to cause them so much pain?

DRIVER: What have I said? I only told them to wait.

MRS KAY: Ronnie, the kids with me today don't know what it is
to *look* at a bar of chocolate. Lemonade Ronnie? Lemonade
never touches their lips. (*We should almost hear the violins*.)
These are the children, Ronnie, that stand outside shop
windows in the pouring rain, looking and longing, but never
getting. Even at Christmas time, when your kids from the
better schools are singing carols, opening presents, these kids
are left, outside, left to wander the cold cruel streets.
RONNIE *is grief-stricken.*
Behind him, in the coach, the KIDS *are stuffing themselves
stupid with sweets, chocolate and lemonade.*
MRS KAY *leaves* RONNIE *to it and climbs on board. As*
RONNIE *turns to board the coach all evidence of sweets and
lemonade immediately disappears.* RONNIE *puts his hand in
his pocket, produces a few quid.*

DRIVER (*to the* KID *on the front seat*): Here y' are son, run to
the shops an' see what sweets y' can get with that.

SUSAN (*leaning across*): What did you say?

MRS KAY: Lied like hell of course.
She gets up and faces the KIDS.

MRS KAY: Now listen everyone. Listen. We'll be setting off for
Conway in a couple of minutes.
Cheers.
Listen. Now, we want everybody to enjoy themselves today
and so I don't want any silly squabbling and I don't want
anybody doing anything dangerous either to yourselves or to
others. That's the only rule we're going to have today, think of
yourselves, but think of others as well.
REILLY *and* DIGGA *come rushing onto the coach.*

REILLY: Miss, we're comin' miss, we're comin' with y' . . .

MRS KAY: Where's the note Brian?

REILLY: He didn't give us one, miss. He's comin' himself. He said
to wait.

REILLY *and* DIGGA *go down the aisle to the back of the coach.*

COLIN: He's coming to keep an eye on us.

SUSAN: To make sure we don't enjoy ourselves.

MRS KAY: Well . . . I' suppose we'll just have to deal with him the best way we can.
MRS KAY sits down, next to CAROL. REILLY *and* DIGGA *are at the back seat.*

REILLY (*to a* LITTLE KID *on the back seat*): Right. You. Move.

LITTLE KID: Why?

REILLY: Cos we claimed the back seat, that's why.

LITTLE KID: You're not even in the Progress though.

DIGGA: 'Ey, hardfaced, we used to be, so shift!

REILLY: Now move before I mince y'.
Unseen by REILLY *and* DIGGA, BRIGGS *has climbed on board. All the* KIDS *spotting a cloud on a blue horizon.* BRIGGS *glaring. Barks suddenly.*

BRIGGS: Reilly, Dickson sit down!

REILLY: Sir we was only . . .

BRIGGS (*stacatto*): I said sit lad, now move.
REILLY *and* DIGGA *sit on the* LITTLE KID *who is forced out. He stands, exposed in the aisle, terrified of* BRIGGS. Sit down. What you doing lad, what you doing?

LITTLE KID: Sir sir sir . . . sir I haven't got a seat. (*Almost in tears.*)

BRIGGS: Well find one, boy, find one!
COLIN *gets out of his seat and indicates the* KID *to sit there.*

BRIGGS (*to* MRS KAY): You've got some real bright sparks here Mrs Kay. A right bunch.

MRS KAY: Well I think we might just manage to survive now that you've come to look after us.

BRIGGS: The boss thought it might be a good idea if you had an extra member of staff. Looking at this lot I'd say he was right. There's a few of them I could sling off right now. (*Barking.*) Linda Croxley, what are you doin'? Sit down girl. (*He addresses all the* KIDS.) Right! Now listen: we wouldn't like you to think that we don't want you to enjoy yourselves today, because we do. But a lot of you won't have been on a school outing before and therefore won't know *how* to enjoy yourselves. So I'll tell you:

*Throughout the last few lines of dialogue we have heard the
intro for 'Instructions on Enjoyment'*

BRIGGS (*sings*):
To enjoy a trip upon a coach
We sit upon our seats
We do not wander up and down the aisles
We do not use obscenities
Or throw each other sweets
We talk politely, quietly nod and smile.
There'll be no shouting on this outing, will there?
(*Screaming*.) WILL THERE?

KIDS: No sir.

BRIGGS: No sir, no sir.
We look nicely through the windows
At the pretty scenery
We do not raise our voices, feet or fists
And I do not, are you listening girl,
I do not want to see
Two fingers raised to passing motorists
To enjoy this treat
Just stay in your seat
Be quiet, be good and behave!

As BRIGGS *finishes the song the* KID *who went to get the
sweets rushes on board loaded with bags.*

KID: I've got them . . . I've got loads . . .

BRIGGS: Where've you been?

KID: Sir, gettin' sweets.

BRIGGS: Sweets? SWEETS!

MRS KAY (*reaching for the sweets*): Thank you Maurice.
The DRIVER *is tapping* BRIGGS *on the shoulder.*

DRIVER: Can I have a word with you?

BRIGGS: Pardon?

DRIVER: In private.
He leads the way off the coach. BRIGGS *follows.*
MRS KAY *gives the sweets to* COLIN *and* SUSAN *who start
to dish them out.*

KIDS: 'Ogh, great', 'Give us one, miss,' 'What about me, sir?'

DRIVER (*outside the coach, to* BRIGGS): The thing is, about
these kids, they're like little souls, lost an' wanderin' the cruel
heartless streets.

The DRIVER *continues his lecture to* BRIGGS *outside the coach as we go back inside.*
COLIN *is at the back seat giving out sweets to* REILLY *and Co.*

REILLY: How are y' gettin' on with miss, sir?

DIGGA: We say y', sir, goin' into that pub with her.
Further down the aisle SUSAN *is watching and listening as she gives out sweets.*

COLIN (*covering his embarrassment*): Did you?

REILLY: Are you in love with her, sir?

COLIN (*making his escape*): All right, you've all got sweets have you?

REILLY (*jeering*): Sir's in love, sir's in love . . .
REILLY *laughing as* COLIN *makes his way back along the aisle.*

SUSAN: Watch it Brian!

REILLY (*feigned innocence*): What, miss?

SUSAN: You know what.

REILLY: Agh, hey, he is in love with y' though, isn't he, miss?

DIGGA: I'll bet he wants to marry y', miss.

REILLY: You'd be better off with me, miss. I'm better lookin', an' I'm sexier.
SUSAN *gives up playing it straight. She goes up to* REILLY *and whispers to him.*

SUSAN: Brian, little boys shouldn't try and act like men. The day might come when their words are put to the test!
She walks away.

REILLY: Any day, miss, any day.

DIGGA: What did she say, what did she say?

REILLY: She said she fancied me!
BRIGGS *and the* DRIVER *come on board.* BRIGGS *goes to sit opposite* MRS KAY.

BRIGGS: Well . . . We've got a right head-case of a driver.
The engine comes to life. The KIDS *cheer.* BRIGGS *gives a warning look. Looks back. As he does so we see a mass of hands raised in two fingered gestures to anyone who might be passing. Simultaneously the* KIDS *sing:*

KIDS:
We're off, we're off
We're off in a motor car

Sixty coppers are after us
An' we don't know where we are
We turned around a corner
Eatin' a Christmas pie
Along came a copper
An' he hit me in the eye.
I went to tell me mother
Me mother wasn't in
I went to tell me Father
An' he kicked me in the bin

Which segues into the 'Travelling Song':

Our day out
Our day out
Our day out

Which fades to:

Our day . . .

The following split between all the KIDS, *each taking a
different line.*

Look at the dogs
Look at the cats
A broken window in Tesco's
Look at the empty Corpy flats

Look at the streets
Look at the houses
Agh look at that feller
With the hole in the back of his trousers

Look at the pushchairs
Look at the prams
Little kids out shoppin'
With their mams.

Oh there's our Tracey
There's my mate
He's missed the bloody bus
Got up too late

Look at the men
All on the dole
Look at the workers
Layin' cable down that hole

Look at the cars
Look there's a train
Look at the clouds
God, I hope it doesn't rain

*Which segues back into the refrain 'Our Day Out', repeated
and fading.*
On the back seat the LITTLE KID *overhears a conversation
between* DIGGA *and* REILLY.

DIGGA: Reilly, light up.

REILLY: Where's Briggsy?

DIGGA: Up the front. Y' all right, I'll keep the eye out for y'.

LITTLE KID: Agh 'ey, you've got ciggies. I'm gonna tell miss.

DIGGA: Tell her. She won't do nothin' anyway.

LITTLE KID: I'll tell sir.

REILLY: You do an' I'll gob y'.

DIGGA: Come on, open that window you.

LITTLE KID: Why?

REILLY: Why d' y' think? So we can get a bit of fresh air.

LITTLE KID: Well there is no fresh air round here. You just want
to smoke. An' smokin' stunts your growth.

REILLY: I'll stunt your bleedin' growth if y' don't get it open.
ANDREWS *gets up and reaches obligingly for the window.*

ANDREWS: I'll open it for y' Reilly.
REILLY *ducks behind a seat and lights up.*

ANDREWS: Gis a ciggie.

REILLY: Sod off. Get y' own ciggies.

ANDREWS: Ah go on, I opened the window for y'.

DIGGA: Be told, y' not gettin' no ciggie. (*Suddenly whispered
to* REILLY:) Briggs! (*As we see* BRIGGS *leave his seat at the
front and head towards the back.*)
REILLY *quickly hands the cigarette to* ANDREWS *who,
unaware of the approaching* BRIGGS, *seizes it with enthusiasm.*

ANDREWS: Ogh . . . thanks Reilly. (*He ducks behind the seat
and takes a massive drag. He comes up to find* BRIGGS *gazing
down at him and the ciggie.*)

BRIGGS: Put it out.

ANDREWS: Sir I wasn't . . .

BRIGGS: Put it out lad. Now get to the front of the coach.
ANDREWS *gets up and makes his way to* BRIGGS' *seat as*
BRIGGS *remains at the back.*
Was it your ciggie, Reilly?

REILLY: Sir, swear on me mother I didn't . . .

DIGGA: Take no notice of him, sir. How can he swear on his

mother, she's been dead ten years.

REILLY *about to stick one on* DIGGA.

BRIGGS: All right. All right! We don't want any argument. There'll be no smokin' if I stay up here will there?

BRIGGS *takes* ANDREWS' *seat. The rest of the coach sing: 'They've all gone quiet at the back', one verse to tune 'She'll Be Coming Round the Mountain'.*

MRS KAY *and* CAROL *are sat next to each other.* CAROL *next to the window staring out of it.*

CAROL: Isn't it horrible eh, miss?

MRS KAY: Mm?

CAROL: Y' know, all the thingy like; the dirt an' that. (*Pause*.) I like them nice places.

MRS KAY: Which places?

CAROL: Know them places on the telly with gardens, an' trees outside an' that.

MRS KAY: You've got trees in Pilot Street, haven't you?

CAROL: They planted some after the riots. But the kids chopped them down an' burnt them on bonfire night. (*Pause*.) Miss . . . miss y' know when I grow up, miss, y' know if I work hard an' learn to read an' write, would you think I'd be able to live in one of them nice places?

MRS KAY (*putting her arm around her*): Well you could try, love, couldn't you, eh?

CAROL: Yeh!

The KIDS *take up the 'Our Day Out' refrain, repeating the line three times.*

On the back seat, REILLY *and* DIGGA, *stifled by* BRIGG's *presence.*

BRIGGS (*suddenly pointing out of the window*): Now just look at that.

DIGGA *and* REILLY *glance but see nothing to look at.*

DIGGA: What?

BRIGGS (*disgusted*): What? Can't you see? Look, those buildings, don't you ever observe what's around you?

REILLY: It's only the docks, sir.

BRIGGS: You don't get buildings like that anymore. Just look at the work that must have gone into that.

REILLY: Do you like it down here then, sir?

BRIGGS: I'm often down here at weekends, taking photographs.

Are you listening, Reilly? There's a wealth of history that won't be here much longer.

REILLY: My old feller used to work down here.

BRIGGS: What did he think of it?

REILLY: He hated it.

BRIGGS: Well you tell him to take another look and he might appreciate it.

REILLY: I'll have a job; I haven't seen him for two years.
REILLY turning away and looking out of the window.
A few seats further down LINDA *suddenly kneeling up on her seat.*

LINDA (*to* JACKIE): Ogh . . . look, there's Sharon (*She shouts and waves.*) Sharon . . . Sha . . .

BRIGGS: Linda Croxley! (*He gets up and moves towards her. Only at the last moment does she turn and sit 'properly'.*) And what sort of an outfit is that supposed to be for a school visit?

LINDA (*chewing and contemptuous, staring out of the window*): What?

BRIGGS: Don't you 'what' me, young lady. (*She merely shrugs.*) You know very well that on school trips you wear school uniform.

LINDA: Well Mrs Kay never said nott'n about it.

BRIGGS: You're not talking to Mrs Kay now.

LINDA: Yeh I know.

BRIGGS (*quietly but threatening*): Now listen here young lady, I don't like your attitude. I don't like it one bit.

LINDA: What have I said? I haven't said nott'n have I?

BRIGGS: I'm talking about your attitude.
She dismisses him with a glance and turns away.
I'm telling you now, miss. Carry on like this and when we get to Conway you'll be spending your time in the coach.

LINDA: I don't care, I don't wanna see no crappy castle anyway.

BRIGGS: Just count yourself lucky you're not a lad. Now I'm warning you. Cause any more unpleasantness on this trip and I shall see to it that it's the last you ever go on. Is that understood? Is it?

LINDA (*sighs*): Yeh.

BRIGGS: It better had be.

He makes his way to the front of the coach and addresses the
KID *next to* ANDREWS.

BRIGGS: Right, you, what's your name? Wake up.

MAURICE: Sir, me?

BRIGGS: What's your name?

MAURICE: McNally, sir.

BRIGGS: Right McNally go and sit at the back.

MAURICE: Sir, I don't like the back.

BRIGGS: Never mind what you like, go and sit at the back.
MAURICE *does so.*
Right, Andrews, shove up.
BRIGGS *sitting by him.*
How long have you been smoking, Andrews?

ANDREWS: Sir, I don't . . . Sir, since I was eight.

BRIGGS: And how old are you now?

ANDREWS: Sir, thirteen, sir.

BRIGGS: What do your parents say?

ANDREWS: Sir, me mam says nothin' about it but when me dad
comes home sir, sir he belts me.

BRIGGS: Because you smoke?

ANDREWS: No sir, because I won't give him one.
Pause.

BRIGGS: Your father works away from home does he?

ANDREWS: What? No, sir.

BRIGGS: You said, 'when he comes home', I thought you meant
he was away a lot.

ANDREWS: He is. But he doesn't go to work.

BRIGGS: Well what does he do then?

ANDREWS: I don't know. Sir, he just comes round every now
an' then an' has a barney with me mam. Then he goes off
again. I think he tries to get money off her but she won't
give him it though. She hates him. We all hate him.

BRIGGS: Listen, why don't you promise yourself you'll give up
smoking? You must realise it's bad for your health.

ANDREWS: Sir, I did sir. I've got a terrible cough.

BRIGGS: Then why don't you pack it in?

ANDREWS: Sir, I can't.

BRIGGS: Thirteen and you can't stop smoking?

ANDREWS: No, sir.

BRIGGS (*sighing and shaking his head*): Well you'd better not let me catch you again.

ANDREWS: No, sir. I won't.

KIDS VARIOUS: There's the tunnel, the Mersey tunnel, we're goin' throu the tunnel . . .
All the KIDS *cheer as the bus goes into the tunnel (probably best conveyed by blackout).*

KIDS (*sing*):
The Mersey tunnel is three miles long
And the roof is made of glass
So that you can drive right in
And watch the ships go past
There's a plug hole every five yards
They open it every night
It lets in all the water and it
Washes away the sha na na na na na na na na . . .

BRIGGS *rising as they are, he thinks, about to sing an obscenity; sitting down again as he fails to catch them at it. The* KIDS *repeat the verse and* BRIGGS *repeats his leap to try and catch them. Again they merely sing 'Sha na na na' etc. They repeat the verse once more. This time* BRIGGS *doesn't leap to his feet as the* KIDS *sing:*
And washes away the shite!
As BRIGGS *leaps to his feet, too late, the* KIDS *are staring from the windows at the 'pretty scenery'.* BRIGGS *stares at them.*

GIRL: Sir, are we in Wales yet?

BOY: Sir, I need to go to the toilet.

BRIGG: Yes, well you should have thought of that before you got on the coach, shouldn't you?

BOY: Sir, I did, sir, I've got a weak bladder.

BRIGGS: Then a little control will help to strengthen it.

MAURICE: Sir, sir I'm wettin' meself.

DIGGA: Are we stoppin' for toilets sir?
Which all the KIDS *take up in one form or another, groans, moans and cries of 'toilet'. 'I wanna go the toilet.'*

BRIGGS: For God's sake. Just shut up, all of you shut up!

MRS KAY: Mr. B . . .

BRIGGS: I said shut up. (*Then realising.*) Erm, sorry sorry. Mrs Kay?

MRS KAY: I would like to go to the toilet myself!
BRIGGS *staring at her.*

MILTON (*hand raised*): Sir . . . Sir . . .

BRIGGS (*snaps*): Yes. Milton.

MILTON: Sir, I wondered if you were aware that over six hundred people per year die from ruptured bladders.

BRIGGS (*seeing he's defeated, turning to the* DRIVER): Pull in at the toilets up ahead will you? (*He turns to the* KIDS.) Right, I want everybody back on this coach in two minutes. Those who need the toilets, off you go.
Most of the KIDS *get off the coach and go off as if to the toilets.*
REILLY, DIGGA *and a small group form some yards away from the coach, obviously smoking.*

COLIN (*approaching them*): All right lads. Shouldn't be too long before we're in Wales.

LITTLE KID: Wales, that's in the country isn't it, sir?

COLIN: A lot of it's countryside yes but . . .

REILLY: Lots of woods eh, sir?

COLIN: Well, woods, yes mountains and lakes.

REILLY: An' you're gonna show miss the woods are y' sir?

COLIN: Just watch it Brian, right?

REILLY: Ah, I only meant was y' gonna show her the plants an' the trees.

COLIN: I know quite well what you meant. (*He turns to go.*) And if I was you I'd put that fag out before you burn your hand. If Mr Briggs catches you you'll spend the rest of the day down at the front of the coach with him and you don't want that to happen do you? Now come on, put it out.
REILLY *puts out the cigarette and* COLIN *walks away.*

REILLY (*shouting after him*): I'll show miss the woods for y' sir.
Throughout the above all the other KIDS *have made their way back onto the coach.*

MRS KAY (*returning*): Come on, Brian, come on . . . (*She ushers them on board.*) O.K. Ronnie, I think that's the lot.
The bus starts.

LITTLE KID: Miss miss . . .

MRS KAY: Yes.

LITTLE KID: Miss I wanna go the toilet.

KIDS: Agh shurrup . . .

DRIVER: Get ready, a humpety backed bridge . . .
As they go over the bridge all passengers are bumped off their seats.

TWO BORED GIRLS (*in unison*):
It's borin'
It's bleedin' borin'.
Another minute here an' I'll be snorin'.
Lookin' at loads of roads, miss
When are we gonna stop?
There's nothin' to do
Only look at the view
An' if you've seen one hill
You've seen the bleedin' lot.

God! It's borin', isn't it borin',
It's borin'
It's bleedin' borin'.

The other KIDS *take up, quietly, the refrain of 'It's borin', it's bleedin' borin'.'*
At the front of the coach MRS KAY *is having a word with* RONNIE.

MRS KAY: Ronnie, I was wondering if there was somewhere we could stop for a little while, have a cup of tea and let them stretch their legs?

DRIVER: All right Mrs Kay, there's a café just up ahead; d' y' want me to pull in?

MRS KAY: Thanks Ron.
The song begins as the KIDS *dismantle the coach and re-set the seats to form the café/shop and picnic area.*
Note: if doubling is necessary the actress playing SUSAN *changes here to play the café/shop proprietress.*

BRIGGS (*sings*):
All right! Let's get this straight.
We're only stopping for a quarter of an hour
When you leave the bus you will get in line and wait
We do not want this visit turning sour.

MRS KAY: It's all right everybody, there will still be lots of time
For you to stretch your legs and let off steam
You're free to leave the bus now but please don't go getting lost.
The shop's that way, for those who want ice cream.
The KIDS *cheering as they set up the shop/café.*

BRIGGS: All right! Now that's enough
You're behaving like a gang of common scruffs.

MRS KAY: By the book, Mr Briggs?

BRIGGS: Yes, why not by the book?
I want them looking tidy.

MRS KAY: That's one thing they'll never look.

BRIGGS: Come on now get in line, I said line up, do what you're told.

MRS KAY: For a straight line is a wonderful thing to behold.
As the music continues as underscoring BRIGGS *addresses the* KIDS.

BRIGGS: Now the people who run these places provide a good and valuable service to travellers like ourselves and so I want to see this place treated with the sort of respect it deserves. Now come on, let's have a straight line, in twos . . .
MRS KAY *at the front of the queue which is being formed. Inevitably there are* KIDS *who don't conform exactly to* BRIGGS' *concept of a straight line.*
Come on you two, get in line. You two! Reilly, get in line lad. I said in line . . .

MRS KAY: Mr Briggs . . .

BRIGGS: I think it's under control Mrs Kay, thank you. (*Barking at* KIDS.) Come on! Cut out the fidgeting. Just stand.
Straight! That's more . . . RONSON. Come here lad.

MRS KAY: Mr Briggs . . .

BRIGGS: It's all right Mrs Kay! (*To* RONSON:) Now just where do you think you are lad?

RONSON (*a beat as he wonders*): Sir . . . Sir, Wales?

BRIGGS (*almost screaming by now*): Get in line lad.

BRIGGS (*sings*):
All right. That's looking fine.
Chaos turned to order in a stroke.

MRS KAY: Quite amazing Mr Briggs, they're standing in a line!

BRIGGS: And it's important Mrs Kay, it's not a joke.

MRS KAY: Oh yes, of course it's awfully serious. I'm terribly impressed
Such achievements are the hallmark of the great
A quite remarkable example of a very straight, straight line
Congratulations Mr Briggs it's . . . well it's straight!

BRIGGS: I think that's good, don't you?

MRS KAY: They do so well at standing two by two.

BRIGGS: They do us credit, Mrs Kay.

MRS KAY: Perhaps that's true,
   If you stake your reputation on a stationary queue!

BRIGGS: Come on, it's better than a rabble, there they are as good as gold,

MRS KAY: Oh, a straight line is a wonderful thing to behold.

BRIGGS (*spoken*): With organisation Mrs Kay, with organisation it can be done.
   MRS KAY, *the other* TEACHERS *and the* KIDS *hitting the song finale as per Hollywood, splitting into two lines, hands waving and legs kicking.*

ALL: A straight line is a wonderful thing to behold!
   And on the last note they are back in twos, lined up.

THE SHOPKEEPER: Right, two at a time.
   The KIDS *charge as one into the shop.*

BRIGGS (*apoplectic*): Stop, I said stop . . . stop . . .
   MRS KAY *takes his arm and diverts him.*

MRS KAY: Oh let's forget about them for a while. Come and have some coffee out of my flask. Come on.
   A sea of KIDS *in front of a sweet counter and a harrassed* SHOPKEEPER.

SHOPKEEPER: Fifty-four, the chocolate bars are fifty-four.

MAURICE: That's robbery.

KID: They're only thirty pence down our way.

GIRL 1: Yeh, an' they're twice the size.

KID: Ey missis, give us one of them up there.
   As she turns her back the KIDS *begin robbing sweets.*

SHOPKEEPER: Hey. Put that down, give that here. Where's your teachers? They should be in here with you.

KID: What for? They couldn't afford to buy anything, the prices you charge.

SHOPKEEPER: There's a surcharge for school parties and if you don't like it you can get out.
   Blackout and freeze as we see BRIGGS *and* MRS KAY *outside,* BRIGGS *reluctant, keeping an eye on the shop.*

MRS KAY: Isn't it nice to get away from them for a few minutes?

BRIGGS: To be quite honest Mrs Kay, I think we should be in there, looking after them.
   Blackout and freeze the TEACHERS.

THE SHOPKEEPER (*amidst the chaos*): 'Ere. Put that down.
Keep your hands to yourselves.

GIRL 2: How much are the Bounties?
The SHOPKEEPER *turns her back and much of the counter
contents goes into the* KIDS' *pockets.*

SHOPKEEPER: Now just a minute, give me that hand. Come on,
put it back.

KID: Y' big robber.

GIRL 1: Ey you, I haven't robbed nottn'.

MILTON: How much are the penny chews?

SHOPKEEPER: Tenpence, the penny chews are tenpence. (*She
clouts a* KID.) Take your 'ands off!

MILTON: But they're called 'penny' chews.

SHOPKEEPER: Yes! They're called penny chews but they cost
tenpence each.

MAURICE: It's robbery that.

MILTON: If the penny chews cost tenpence each don't you think
they should be called tenpenny chews?

SHOPKEEPER: But they're not called tenpenny chews. They're
called penny chews and they cost tenpence! Right?

MILTON: I hope you realise this represents a serious breach of
the Trades Description Act.

SHOPKEEPER: And I hope you realise that if you don't shut up
there'll be a serious breach of your bloody head!

RONSON: D' y' sell chips?

SHOPKEEPER: NO!
Blackout and freeze the shop.

MRS KAY *and* BRIGGS *outside the café.*

BRIGGS: There's not just our school to think of, you know. What
about those who come after us? They're dependent on the
goodwill of the people who run these places.

MRS KAY: Considering the profit they make from the kids I
don't think they've got too much to complain about.
KIDS *are beginning to emerge from the shop/café moaning
about the prices and dismissing the place.*
Mr Briggs. I didn't ask you to come on this trip.

BRIGGS: No, but the headmaster did.
*Throughout the following song the coach is reassembled. By
the end of the song everyone is sat in his or her seat and the
coach is on its way again.*

KIDS (*sing*):
> Penny chews are tenpence in this caff
> Yes penny chews are tenpence in this caff
> They say prices are inflated
> But it's robbery, let's face it
> When penny chews are tenpence, what a laugh.
>
> They're chargin' stupid prices for their sweets
> Yes they're chargin' stupid prices for their sweets
> An' they must be makin' quids
> Out of all poor starvin' kids
> Cause they're chargin' stupid prices for their sweets
>
> No they shouldn't be allowed to charge that much
> They shouldn't be allowed to charge that much
> It's robbery it's last it's
> Just a bunch of thievin' bastards
> Who think that everyone they meet's an easy touch.
>
> Well it would have cost us more than we have got
> Yes it would have cost us more than we have got
> Why swindle an' defraud it?
> When they know we can't afford it
> It's a good job that we robbed the bleedin' lot!

COLIN, *who has been sitting with* BRIGGS, *gets up to check that everything is OK. As he gets near* LINDA*'s seat her mate* JACKIE *taps her on the shoulder and points him out.* LINDA *turning and smiling at* COLIN.

LINDA: Sir, are y' comin' to sit by me, are y'?

JACKIE: Don't sit by her, sir, come an' sit by me.

COLIN: I've got my seat down at the front thanks Jackie.

LINDA: Here, sir.

COLIN: What Linda?

LINDA: Come here, I wanna tell y' somethin'.

COLIN: Well go on.

LINDA: Ah hey sir. I don't want everyone to hear. Come on, just sit here while I tell y'.

JACKIE: Go on sir, she won't bite y'.

LINDA: Come on.
> COLIN *reluctantly sits.* JACKIE*'s head poked through the space between the seats.*

COLIN: Well? What is it?
> *They laugh.*
> You're not going to tell me a joke are you?

They laugh.

Look Linda, I'll have to go I've . . .

LINDA (*quickly links her arm through his and holds him there*):
No sir, listen, listen. She said I wouldn't tell y', but I will.
Sir, sir I think you're lovely.

COLIN (*quickly getting up*): Linda! (*And returns to his seat next
to* BRIGGS.)

LINDA: I told him. I said I would. Oh God he's boss him isn't
he eh?

JACKIE: Oh go way you. You've got no chance. He's goin' with
miss.

LINDA: He might chuck her. Might start goin' with me. Might
marry me.

JACKIE (*shrieking*): Oh don't be mental. You'll never get a
husband like sir. You'll end up marryin' someone like your
old feller.

LINDA: You're just jealous girl.

JACKIE: Get lost.

LINDA *turns and dismisses her, stares out of the window and
begins to sing.*

LINDA: I'm in love with sir
But sir doesn't care
Cos sir's in love with her
Over there
With the hair
It isn't fair

She turns to JACKIE.

If I was the wife of a man like sir
My life would not be full of trouble and care
I'd look forward to the nights and we'd make a perfect pair
Me and sir

I'm in love with sir
But sir doesn't care
Cos sir's in love with her
Over there
With the hair
It isn't fair

If I could marry sir I'd be all right.
I wouldn't need to work and we would stay in every night
We'd have some lovely holidays and I would wash his collars
Really white

THE KIDS: She's in love with sir
    Bur sir doesn't care
    Cos sir's in love with her
    Over there
    With the hair
    It isn't fair

JACKIE: You'll be the wife of a man like your dad
    He'll disappear when you grow fat
    You'll be left with the kids and you'll live in a
    council flat

THE KIDS: She's in love with sir
    But sir doesn't care
    Cos sir's in love with her
    Over there
    With the hair
    It isn't fair

LINDA: I'm in love with sir.
    MRS KAY *is talking to the* DRIVER. *She returns to her seat next to* CAROL.

BRIGGS (*to* COLIN *who is sat next to him*): You know what Mrs Kay's problem is, don't you?

COLIN (*trying to keep out of it*): Mm?

BRIGGS: Well! She thinks I can't see through all this woolly-minded liberalism. You know what I mean? All right (GIRLS 1 *and* 2, LITTLE KID *and* MAURICE *arguing about sweets,* BRIGGS *machine gunning a 'Be quiet' at them.*) I mean, she has her methods and I have mine but this setting herself up as the champion of the non-academics! I mean, it might look like love and kindness but it doesn't fool me. And it doesn't do kids a scrap of good. I think you've got to risk being disliked if you're going to do anything for kids like these. They've got enough freedom at home haven't they? Eh? With their five quid pocket money and telly till all hours, video games and that. Eh? I don't know about you, I don't know about you but to me her philosophy's all over the place. (*Pause.*) Eh?

COLIN (*reluctant but having to answer*): Actually I don't think it's got anything to do with a formulated philosophy.

BRIGGS: You mean you've not noticed all this anti-establishment, just-let-the-kids-roam-wild, don't check 'em sort of attitude?

COLIN: Of course I've noticed. But she's like this all the time. This trip isn't organised on the basis of any profound theory.

BRIGGS: Well what's the method she does work to then? Mm? Eh? I mean, you know her better than me, go on you tell me.

COLIN: Well . . . she, for one thing, she likes them.

BRIGGS: Who?

COLIN: The kids. She likes kids.

BRIGGS: What's that got to do with it?

COLIN (*pause*): The principle behind this trip is that the kids should have a good day out.

BRIGGS: And isn't that what I'm saying? But if they're going to have a good and stimulating day it's got to be better planned and executed than this . . .
BRIGGS suddenly noticing that they have turned off the expected route.
What's this? Where are we going? This isn't . . .

MRS KAY: Oh it's all right Mr Briggs. I've checked with the driver, we thought it might be a good idea if we called in at the zoo for an hour. We've got plenty of time.

BRIGGS: But, this trip was arranged so that we could visit Conway Castle.

MRS KAY: Ooh, we're going there as well. I know you're very fond of ruins. Now listen everyone, as an extra bonus, we've decided to call in here at the zoo.
Cheers.

BRIGGS: But look, we can't . . .

MRS KAY: Now the rest of the staff will be around if you want to know anything about the various animals, although it's not much good asking me because I don't know one monkey from the next . . .

BRIGGS: Mrs Kay . . .

MRS KAY (*ignoring him*): But, Progress Class, we're very lucky today to have Mr Briggs with us, because Mr Briggs is something of an expert in natural history. He's something of a David Bellamy, aren't you, Mr Briggs? So if you want to know more about the animals, ask Mr Briggs. Now come on. Leave your things on the coach.
The underscoring for 'Who's Watching Who?' begins as the TEACHERS set up the Zoo and café.
The KIDS spread out in groups around the auditorium as though at different parts of the zoo.

KIDS (*singing as they move*):
Sealions and penguins
Drums.
Swimming in the zoo
Drums.
What do seals eat?
Drums.
Pilchard sarnies
Who's watching who's watching who's watching who?
Who's watching who's watching who's watching who?
Centipedes and pythons
Wriggling at the zoo
What do snakes eat?
Wrigleys spearmint
Who's watching who's watching etc.
Middle eight:
Elephants from Africa, an Aussie Kangaroo
All flown in on jumbo jets and stuck here in the zoo
The two BORED GIRLS *enter and speak with drums underscoring their verse.*

BORED GIRLS: It's borin'
It's bleedin' borin'
The lions are all asleep
they're not even roarin'.
It's just a load of parrots
Bleedin' monkeys an' giraffes,
It isn't worth a carrot
I come here for a laugh
But it's borin'
It's really borin'
We shoulda stayed at school
An' done some drawin'
A zoo's just stupid animals
An' some of them are smelly
I think zoo's are better
When y' watch them on the telly.
It's borin'
Bleedin' borin' . . .
As they close their verse the other KIDS *take up the song again.*

Coloured birds in cages
Do you want to fly away?
What do birds eat?
Sir, bird's custard.
Who's watching who's watching etc.

BRIGGS *and a group of* KIDS *enter and look down into the bear pit.*

BRIGGS: And a brown bear is an extremely dangerous animal. You see those claws, they could leave a really nasty mark.

ANDREWS: Could it kill y' sir?

BRIGGS: Well why do you think they keep it in a pit?

RONSON: I think that's cruel sir. Don't you?

BRIGGS: Not if it's treated well, no. Don't forget, Ronson that an animal like this would have been born into captivity. It's always had walls around it so it won't know anything other than this sort of existence, will it?

RONSON: I'll bet it does.

GIRL 2: How do you know? Sir's just told you hasn't he? If it was born in a cage an' it's lived all it's life in a cage well it won't know any different will it? So it won't want anything different.

RONSON: Well why does it kill people then?

ANDREWS: What's that got to do with it, dick head?

RONSON: It kills people because people are cruel to it. They keep it in here, in this pit so when it gets out it's bound to go mad an' want to kill people. Can't y' see?

ANDREWS: Sir he's thick. Tell him to shuttup.

RONSON: I'm not thick. Even if it has lived all its life in there it must know musn't it sir?

BRIGGS: Know what Ronson?

RONSON: Know about other ways of livin'. About bein' free. Sir it only kills people cos they keep it trapped in here but if it was free an' it was treated all right it'd start to be friends with y' then wouldn't it? If y' were doin' nothing wrong to it it wouldn't want to kill y'.

BRIGGS: Well I wouldn't be absolutely sure about that, Ronson.

ANDREWS: Sir's right. Bears kill y' cos it's in them to kill y'.

GIRL 1: Ah come on sir, let's go to the Pets Corner.

ANDREWS: No way sir, let's see the big ones.

BRIGGS: We'll get round them all eventually.

GIRL 1: Come on the sir, let's go the pets corner . . .
　　GIRL 1 *and* GIRL 2 *go to link* BRIGGS' *arms. He shrugs them off.*

BRIGGS: Now walk properly, properly . . .

GIRL 1: Agh hey sir, all the other teachers let y' link them.
　　MRS KAY *enters with another group of* KIDS. *She has got* KIDS *on either side, linking her arms.*

MRS KAY: How are you getting on? Plying you with questions?

BRIGGS: Yes, yes they've been . . . very good.

MRS KAY: I'm just going for a cup of coffee. Want to join me?

BRIGGS: Well I was just on my way to the Pets Corner . . .

ANDREWS: It's all right sir, we'll go on our own.

MRS KAY: Oh come on, they'll be all right.

BRIGGS: But can these people be trusted Mrs Kay?

MRS KAY: They'll be all right. Colin and Susan are walking round. And the place is walled in.

ANDREWS: Go on sir, you go an' have a cuppa. You can trust us.

BRIGGS: Ah can I though? If I go off for a cup of tea with Mrs Kay, can you people be trusted to act responsibly?

KIDS: Yes sir.

JIMMY: Sir what sort of bird's that sir?

BRIGGS: Erm. Oh let me see, yes it's a macaw.

MRS KAY: Come on.

BRIGGS (*following* MRS KAY): They're very good talkers.
　　MRS KAY *and* BRIGGS *off.*

KEVIN: I told y' it wasn't a parrot.

JIMMY (*trying to get the bird to talk*): Liverpool, Liverpool. Come on say it, y' dislocated sparrow.

KIDS (*sing*):
　　Mountain lions and panthers
　　Leopards in the zoo
　　What do lions eat?

JIM: ⎱
KEV: ⎰ Evertonians

KIDS: Who's watching who's watching, who's watching who? Who's watching who's watching who's watching who?

　　MRS KAY *and* BRIGGS *sitting as if in the café, two teas and a couple of cakes.* KIDS *as though looking through the windows of the café.*

KIDS: Teachers in the café
Takin' tea for two
What do they eat

SPOKEN: Ogh, chocolate cream cakes!
BRIGGS *and* MRS KAY *suddenly noticing hungry eyes on their cakes.*

MRS KAY (*waving them away*): Ogh go on, go away ... shoo ...

KIDS (*dispersing and going off singing*):
Who's watching who's watching who's watching who
Who's watching who's watching who's watching who?

BRIGGS: Another tea Mrs Kay?

MRS KAY: Oh call me Helen. Do you know I loathe being called Mrs Kay. Do you know I tried to get the kids to call me by my first name. I told them, call me Helen, not Mrs Kay. They were outraged. They wouldn't do it. So it's good old Mrs Kay again. Oh, no, no more tea thanks.

BRIGGS: They're really quite interested, the kids, aren't they?

MRS KAY: In the animals, oh yes. And it's such a help having you here because you know so much about this sort of thing.

BRIGGS: Well I wouldn't say I was an expert but ... you know, perhaps when we're back at school I could come along to your department and show some slides I've got.

MRS KAY: Would you really? Oh Mr Briggs, we'd love that.

BRIGGS: Well look, I'll sort out which free periods I've got and we'll organise it for then.
COLIN *and* SUSAN *approaching.*
The KIDS *quickly lined up in the sort of orderly queue* BRIGGS *would approve of.*

SUSAN: Ready when you are.

MRS KAY: Are they all back?

SUSAN: It's amazing, we came around the corner and they're all there, lined up waiting to get on the bus.

MRS KAY: Wonders will never cease.

BRIGGS: OK. (*Sees the* KIDS.) Well look at this Mrs Kay, they're learning at last eh? Right, all checked and present? On board then ...
The KIDS *go to climb aboard just as an* ANIMAL KEEPER *all polo-neck and wellies, rushes towards them.*

KEEPER: Hold it right there.

MRS KAY: Hello, have we forgotten something?

KEEPER: Are you supposed to be in charge of this lot?

MRS KAY: Why, what's the matter?

KEEPER: Children? They're not bloody children, they're animals. It's not the zoo back there, this is the bloody zoo, here.

BRIGGS: Excuse me! Would you mind controlling your language and telling me what's going on?

KEEPER (*ignores him, pushes past and confronts the* KIDS): Right, where are they?
Innocent faces and replies of 'What?', 'Where's what?'

KEEPER: You know bloody well what . . .

BRIGGS (*intercepting him*): Now look, this has just gone far enough. Would you . . .
He is interrupted by the loud clucking of a hen.
The KEEPER *strides up to a* KID *and pulls open his jacket. A bantam hen is revealed.*

KEEPER (*taking the hen, addresses the other* KIDS): Right, now I want the rest.
There is a moment's hesitation before the floodgates are opened. Animals appear from every conceivable hiding-place.
BRIGGS *glares as the animals are rounded up.*
The KIDS *stay in place, waiting for the thunder.*

BRIGGS: I trusted you lot. And this is the way you repay me. (*Pause as he fights to control his anger.*) I trusted all of you but it's obvious that trust is something you know nothing about.

RONSON: Sir we only borrowed them.

BRIGGS (*screaming*): Shut up lad! Is it any wonder that people won't do anything for you? The moment we start to treat you like real people, what happens? Well that man was right. You act like animals, animals.

MRS KAY: Come on now, take the animals back.
The KIDS *relieved at finding a way to go. As they move off* BRIGGS *remains.*

BRIGGS: And that's why you're treated like animals, why you'll always be treated like animals.

KIDS (*sing very quietly as they exit*):
Our day out
Our day out

BRIGGS (*alone on stage*): ANIMALS!
Blackout.

ACT TWO

TEACHERS *and* KIDS *outside Conway Castle.*

BRIGGS: We'll split into four groups Mrs Kay. Each member of
staff will be responsible for one group. It will take approxi-
mately one and a quarter hours to tour the castle and at
three-fifteen we will reassemble at the coach. Walk round in
twos, and I mean walk! Right, my group, this way . . .
The others going off. The KIDS *in* BRIGGS' *group following
him with little enthusiasm.*

BRIGGS (*pointing up at the castle walls*): Now, those large
square holes just below the battlements: long planks of wood
were supported there and that's where the archers would fire
from if the castle was under attack. Something really
interesting up there is, if you look at that tower, you'll see
that it's not quite perpendicular. What does perpendicular
mean?

MAURICE: I don't know.

MILTON: Sir, sir . . .

BRIGGS: Yes?

MILTON: Sir, straight up.
Sniggers from the other KIDS.

BRIGGS: Are you listening lad? You might just learn something.
Music intro for 'Castle Song'. BRIGGS *sings:*
I find it so depressing
I just can't understand
Your failure to appreciate
A thing so fine and grand
Your heritage, your history
You can touch it with your hand
The Yanks have nothing like it

MILTON: Sir, but they've got Disneyland.

BRIGGS (*spoken*): Disneyland.
(*Sings*):
That's not the same at all, this is history, this is real
It should make you feel so proud, so thrilled, so awed
Just standing here for centuries, how does that make you feel?

KIDS: Sir it makes us feel dead bored.

BRIGGS (*music continuing as underscoring*): Bored! Yes and
you'll be bored forever; do you want to know why? Because
you put nothing in. You invest in nothing. And if you invest in

nothing you get nothing in return. This way. Come on, quickly, move.

As BRIGGS *leads his group off,* REILLY *and* DIGGA *slip away from it and get the ciggies out. They hide though when they hear* COLIN *approaching.* LINDA *and* JACKIE *are with him.*

COLIN (*sings*):
Now though these walls are very thick
In places fifteen feet
Just think how cold it must have been
With no real form of heat
Even in the summertime
It must have been quite cold

LINDA: I wonder how they managed, sir,
To keep warm in days of old.

LINDA: Tell us sir go on,
JACKIE: Tell us everything you know
We want to learn from you sir
Yes we do, Ooh Ooh
We really think you're great sir
Tell us everything you know
We'd be really brainy sir,
If all the teachers were like you.

COLIN: Well. They'd obviously . . . where's everybody else gone? Where are the others?

JACKIE: Sir they kept droppin' out as you were talkin'.

COLIN: Oh God!

LINDA: Oh it's all right sir, we're dead interested. Y' can keep showin' us around.

COLIN (*sighs*): All right, what was I saying?

LINDA: You were tellin' us how they kept warm in the olden days.

COLIN: Well for one thing . . . Linda
(*Sings*:) They wore much thicker clothing

LINDA: Even damsels in distress?

COLIN: I expect they *all* had more sense
Than to walk around half-dressed.

GIRLS: We seen this movie once sir,
Where they had some better ways
To keep each other cosy sir,
Back in them olden days.

COLIN (*spoken*): All right Linda, all right . . .

GIRLS: Tell us sir go on
Tell us everything you know
We want to learn from you sir
Yes we do, Ooh Ooh.
We really think you're great sir
Tell us everything you know
We'd be really brainy sir,
If all the teachers were like you.

LINDA: Sir it's dead spooky here. Sir I think it's haunted.
She grabs his arm.

COLIN: Don't be silly.
She throws her arms around him.

LINDA: I'm frightened.

COLIN: Don't do that Linda.

LINDA: But I'm frightened. (*Holding tight.*)

JACKIE (*also grabbing him*): Sir, so am I.

COLIN (*freeing himself*): Now girls, stop being silly. Stop it!
(*Sings:*)
There's nothing to be frightened of
There's no such things as ghosts
Just look how this position
Gives a clear view of the coast

GIRLS: But we'd rather look at you sir

COLIN: Yes, but girls, you're here to learn

GIRLS: Oh sir, you're so impressive when
You behave so strong and firm

Tell us sir, go on
Then we won't be scared at all
We feel so warm and safe when we're with you, Ooh Ooh
We know you will protect us sir
Cos you're all strong and tall
And if we can't believe in ghosts
We can still believe in you

DIGGA *and* REILLY *lean out unnoticed from their hiding
position they touch the* GIRLS *who scream and grab* COLIN
again.

LINDA: It touched me.

COLIN: What did?

LINDA: Oh it did.
REILLY *and* DIGGA *jeering and running off.*

COLIN: God. Come on, girls, come on.

They follow him.

CAROL *is sitting on the battlements, looking out over the estuary. Nearby, on a bench,* MRS KAY *is sitting back enjoying the sun.*

MRS KAY: Why don't you go and have a look around the castle, Carol? You haven't seen it yet.

CAROL: Miss, I don't like it. It's horrible. I'd rather sit here with you an' look at the lake.

MRS KAY: That's the sea.

CAROL: Yeh that's what I mean.

ANDREWS (*runs on and joins them*): Miss, miss I just thought of this great idea; miss wouldn't it be smart if we had somethin' like this castle round our way. The kids wouldn't get into trouble, would they, if they had somewhere like this to play.

CAROL: Miss, we couldn't have somethin' like this round our way, could we?

MRS KAY: Why not?

CAROL: Cos if we had somethin' like this we'd only wreck it wouldn't we?

ANDREWS: No we wouldn't.

CAROL: We would. That's why we never have nothin' nice round our way — we'd smash it up. The corporation knows that an' so why should they waste their time and money. They'd give us nice things if we looked after them, but we don't do we?

ANDREWS: Miss, d' y' know what I think about it miss?

MRS KAY: Go on John, what?

ANDREWS: Miss, miss if all this belonged to us — like it wasn't the corporation's but it was something that we owned, well we wouldn't let no one wreck it would we? Eh? We'd look after it wouldn't we? Defend it. D' y' know what I mean, miss?

MRS KAY: Yes, I think I do. (BRIGGS *enters.*) What you're saying . . .

BRIGGS: Right. You two, off. Go on move.

CAROL: Sir where?

BRIGGS: Anywhere girl. Just move. I want to talk to Mrs Kay. Well come on then.

The two KIDS *reluctantly wander off.* BRIGGS *waiting until they are out of hearing.*

MRS KAY (*quietly angry*): I was talking to those children.

BRIGGS: Yes, an' I'm talking to you, Mrs Kay. This has got to stop.

MRS KAY: Pardon me. What's got to stop?

BRIGGS: What! Can't you see what's going on? It's a shambles, the whole ill-organised affair. Just look what they did at the zoo. Look.
As a group of KIDS *run past playing chase and tick.*
They're just left to race and chase and play havoc. God knows what the castle authorities must think. Now look, when you bring children like this into this sort of environment you can't afford to just let them roam free.
KIDS *rushing past.*
They're just like town dogs let off the leash in the country. My God, for some of them it's the first time they've been further than Birkenhead.

MRS KAY (*quietly*): I know. And I was just thinking; It's a shame really isn't it? We bring them out to a crumbling pile of bricks and mortar and they think they're in the fields of heaven.

BRIGGS: You *are* on their side aren't you?

MRS KAY: Absolutely Mr Briggs, absolutely.
A couple of KIDS *shouting to try and hear the echo of their names.*

BRIGGS: Look, all I want to know from you is what you're going to do about this chaos?

MRS KAY: Well I'd suggest that if you want the chaos to stop you should simply look at it not as chaos but what it actually is — kids, with a bit of space around them, making a bit of noise. All right, so the head asked you to come along — but can't you just relax? There's no point in pretending that a day out to Wales is going to be of some great educational benefit to them. It's too late for them. Most of these kids were rejects the day they came into the world. We're not going to solve anything today Mr Briggs. Can't we just give them a good day out? Mm? At least we could try and do that.

BRIGGS: Well that's a fine attitude isn't it? That's a fine attitude for a member of the teaching profession.

MRS KAY (*beginning to let her temper go*): Well what's your alternative? Eh? Pretending? Pretending that they've got some sort of a future ahead of them? Even if you cared for these kids you couldn't help to make a future for them. You won't educate them because nobody wants them educating.

BRIGGS: Listen Mrs Kay . . .

MRS KAY: No you listen Mr Briggs, you listen and perhaps you'll stop fooling yourself. Teach them? Teach them what? You'll never teach them because nobody knows what to do with them. Ten years ago you could teach them to stand in a line, you could teach them to obey, to expect little more than a lousy factory job. But now they haven't even got that to aim for. Mr Briggs, you won't teach them because you're in a job that's designed and funded to fail! There's nothing for them to do, any of them; most of them were born for factory fodder, but the factories have closed down.

BRIGGS: And I suppose that's the sort of stuff you've been pumping into their minds.

MRS KAY (*laughing*): And you really think they'd understand?

BRIGGS: I'm not going to spend any more time arguing with you. You may have organised this visit, but I'm the one who was sent by the headmaster to supervise. Now, either you take control of the children in your charge or I'll be forced to abandon this visit and order everyone home.

MRS KAY: Well . . . that's your decision. But I'm not going to let you prevent the kids from having some fun. If you want to abandon this visit you'd better start walking because we're not going home. We're going down to the beach!
She walks away.
Colin, round everybody up. Come on everybody, we're going to the beach.

BRIGGS: The beach?

KIDS *and other* TEACHERS *entering as we hear the intro for a song.* MRS KAY *calling to* BRIGGS.

MRS KAY: You can't come all the way to the seaside and not pay a visit to the beach.

KIDS (*singing to the tune of the 'Mersey Tunnel Song'. As they sing they set up the rocks and the beach*):
The castle's just a load of stones
It's borin' and it's dead
Can't even fire the cannons
Cos they're blocked off at the end
So we're goin' to the seashore
An' miss says we can
Build a better castle there
With just the bloody sand

Continue underscoring as KIDS *begin to whip off shoes and socks,* MRS KAY *doing the same. The* BORED GIRLS *firmly keeping their shoes and socks on.*

BORED GIRLS: It's borin'
It's bleedin' borin'
It's only a load of sand
An' seagulls squawkin'

BORED 1: God, we've been here bloody hours
Can't we go home yet?

BORED 2: Look at the water

BORED 1: Water's borin'
All it does is make y' wet

BOTH: Yeh it's borin'
Really borin'.

KIDS: We're gonna find some thingies
In the pools and in the rocks
We're gonna shout an' run about
Without our shoes and socks

They do until almost as one the immensity of the place hits them. They each stand, transfixed, looking out to sea and squelching their toes in the wet sand.
Music slow and wave-like.

The sea's gi-bleedin-gantic
It must be really wide
Cos we can't even see
What's over on the other side

The sound of the ocean.
DRIVER *running on with a ball.*

DRIVER: Mrs Kay, all right if I take some of them off for a game of footie?

MRS KAY: Yes.

CAROL (*tugging at* MRS KAY*'s sleeve as some of the* KIDS *rush off with* RONNY): Miss, when do we have to go home?

MRS KAY: What's the matter love? Aren't you enjoying yourself?

CAROL: Yeh. But I don't wanna go home. I wanna stay here.

MRS KAY: Carol love, we're here for at least another hour yet. Now why don't you start enjoying yourself instead of worrying about going home.

CAROL: Cos I don't wanna go home.

MRS KAY: Carol love, we have to go home in the end. This is a special day. It can't be like this all the time.

CAROL: Why not?

MRS KAY (*looks at her and sighs. Puts her arm around her*): I don't know, love. Come on, let's go and play football with the others.

CAROL: Nah. (*She breaks away and wanders off.*)
MRS KAY watching her for a moment and then turning to the two BORED GIRLS.

MRS KAY: Come on you two; let's go and play football.

BORED 1: Miss what for?

MRS KAY: What for? Oh, you don't like football. (*Suddenly mimicking them.*) Football's borin', it's dead borin', it's borin' borin' borin'.
They look at her as though she's lost a screw.

BORED 1: We like football.

MRS KAY: Well come on then.
MRS KAY beginning to go.
Come on.

BORED 2: Miss where?

MRS KAY (*almost screaming*): To play football, you said you liked football. Well?

BORED 1: We do on the telly!

BORED 2: Don't like playin' it though. Playin' football's dead . . .
MRS KAY, hands outstretched to throttle them both, rushing at them, and the two GIRLS *suddenly moving. The* GIRLS *being chased off by* MRS KAY.
COLIN, SUSAN, LINDA, JACKIE and other GIRLS *are examining the rock pools.* REILLY, DIGGA *and a small group of followers are having a smoke behind some large rocks.*
REILLY *comes out from behind the rocks and shouts over to* SUSAN.

REILLY: All right, miss?

COLIN (*quietly*): Here we go.

ANDREWS (*to* REILLY): Gis a drag.

DIGGA: Buy your own.

ANDREWS: Don't be a rat. Come on.
REILLY holds out the butt. ANDREWS *goes to take it but before he can,* REILLY *drops it into the sand and treads on it.*

REILLY (*shouting across*): Y' comin' for a walk with me, miss?

COLIN (*standing and shouting back*): Look I'm warning you Reilly . . .

SUSAN: Leave it . . .

COLIN: I'm just about sick of him.

SUSAN: Well go over and have a word with him.

COLIN: I've tried that but whatever I do I can't seem to get through to friend Brian.

SUSAN: I wonder if I could.

REILLY (*shouting over*): What are y' scared of, miss?

SUSAN (*to* COLIN): You go back with the others.

COLIN: What are you going to . . .

SUSAN: Go on . . .

   COLIN *and the group of* GIRLS *begin to move away.*

LINDA: Is miss gonna sort him out, sir?

JACKIE: He needs sortin' out doesn't he, sir?

LINDA: He's all right really y' know, sir. He's great when y' get him on his own.

JACKIE: Oh! An' how do you know?

LINDA: I just do.

   They go off and SUSAN *begins to walk towards* REILLY, *slow and determined, staring straight at him, provocative.* REILLY*'s smile begins to disappear and he gulps for air.* SUSAN *steps straight up to him, pins him against the rocks.*

SUSAN (*husky*): Well Brian . . . I'm here.

REILLY: 'Ey miss.

SUSAN: I'm all yours . . . handsome . . . sexy . . . Brian!

REILLY: Don't mess miss.

SUSAN (*putting her arms around him*): I'm not messing, Big Boy. I'm very, very serious.

   BRIGGS *suddenly enters, sees what he thinks is happening, turns and exits again.* SUSAN *unaware of him.*

SUSAN: What's wrong?

REILLY: I was only havin' a laugh, miss.

SUSAN: You mean . . . don't tell me you weren't being serious, Brian.

REILLY: I was only jokin' with y', miss.

SUSAN (*dropping the act*): Now you listen to me Brian Reilly, you're a handsome lad, but I suggest that in future you stay in your own league, instead of trying to take on ladies who could break you into little pieces. All right? We'll leave it at that shall we?

REILLY: Yes, miss.

She smiles at him, touches his arm affectionately and turns to walk away.

As she does so a pile of jeering faces appear from behind the rocks where they've been hiding and listening.

SUSAN (*turning back*): Clear off all of you. Go and play football or something. I said go!

They do.

Brian.

She motions him to join her. He does.

You know what I was saying about leagues? Well have you ever thought about whose league Linda's in?

REILLY: Linda Croxley? She doesn't fancy me. She's mad about sir. No one else can get a look in.

SUSAN: I wouldn't be too sure about that.

(*Sings.*) I know you like her

    Yes you do, you know you do

    I can't be sure but

    I think that she likes you

REILLY: Ah go way, miss. You're nuts.

SUSAN: Maybe, if you asked her

    Out one night, she'd like to go

    Anyway, no harm done

    The worst thing she can say is 'no'.

REILLY: No chance.

SUSAN: Perhaps you think you'd never stand a chance with her

    Maybe never ever get a second glance from her

    So where the hell's your confidence

    All you need's a bit of nerve

REILLY: I'm no good at . . .

SUSAN: Don't put yourself down

    Can't you see you're not so bad (*She gives him her compact mirror.*)

    Take a look at your reflection

    There you'll see a handsome lad

    REILLY, *smiling and flattered.*

SUSAN: Perhaps you think you'd never stand a chance with her

    Maybe never even get a second glance from her

    So where the hell's your confidence

    All you need's a bit of nerve.

    I know you like her

    Yes you do, you know you do

I can't be sure but
I think that she likes you (*Repeat.*) She likes you.

SUSAN: See you Brian.

REILLY: See y' miss.

He turns and walks to his mates. They begin jeering and laughing but he stands smiling and proud.

REILLY: Well! At least I'm not like you ugly gets. *I* . . . am handsome!

More jeers.

RONNY, MRS KAY *and the* FOOTBALLERS *rush on playing and* REILLY *and the others join the game.*

MRS KAY (*as* REILLY *scores and she gives up being goalie*): Whoooh. I've had enough, I'm all in.

MAURICE: Ah miss, we've got no goalie now.

MRS KAY: Carol can go in goal. (*To* SUSAN *and* COLIN *who are just approaching.*) Where is she?

SUSAN: Who?

KIDS *all exit.*

MRS KAY: Carol, I thought she was with you.

COLIN: We haven't seen her for hours.

MRS KAY: I thought . . . You haven't seen her at all?

SUSAN: We thought she was here.

MRS KAY (*looking around*): Oh, she couldn't, could she?

SUSAN: Lost?

MRS KAY: Don't say it. Perhaps he's seen her. (*Shouting across to* BRIGGS.) Mr Briggs . . . Mr Briggs . . .
BRIGGS *enters.*

BRIGGS: Is that it then? Are we going home?

MRS KAY: Have you seen Carol Chandler in the last hour?

BRIGGS: I thought I'd made it quite plain that I was having nothing more to do with your outing.

MRS KAY: Have you seen Carol Chandler?

BRIGGS: No, I haven't.

MRS KAY: I think she may have wandered off somewhere.

BRIGGS: You mean you've lost her?

MRS KAY: No. I mean she might have wandered off somewhere!

BRIGGS: Well what's that if it's not losing her? All I can say is it's a wonder you haven't lost half a dozen of them.
He turns to go.

COLIN: Listen Briggs, It's about time someone told you what a berk you . . .

BRIGGS (*wheels on him*): And you listen! Sonny! Don't you try to tell me a thing, because you haven't even earned the right. Don't you worry, when we get back to school your number's up, as well as hers (MRS KAY.) And you (SUSAN.) Yes. I saw what was going on between you and Reilly. When we get back I'll have the lot of you.

MRS KAY: Would you mind postponing your threats until we find Carol Chandler? At the moment I'd say the most important thing is to find the girl.

BRIGGS: Don't you mean *try* and find her?

MRS KAY: Susan, you keep the rest of them playing football. We'll split up and look for her.
They go off in separate directions.
We see CAROL. *She is standing on a cliff, looking out, waving at seagulls.*
She sings:
Why can't it always be this way?
Why can't it last for more than just a day?
The sun in the sky and the seagulls flying by
I think I'd like to stay
Then it could always be this way

Why can't it always be like this?
I can't think of anything back home that I would miss
Suppose there'd be a fuss if I wasn't on the bus
But it really would be bliss
If it could always be like this

Shouting to the seagulls,
Seagulls say 'hello'
Wonder how they stay up there so high
Looking at the seashore miles and miles below
Makes me wish that I could fly

Why can't we just stay where we are?
Far far away from the muck and motor cars
If I close my eyes and try and try and try
And wish upon a star,
Then we could all just stay where we are.

As the song ends, BRIGGS *appears on the cliffs and sees* CAROL.

BRIGGS: Carol Chandler, just come here. Who gave you permission to come on these cliffs?

CAROL (*moving to the edge*): No one.
She turns and dismisses him.

BRIGGS: I'm talking to you Miss Chandler.
She continues to ignore his presence.
Now just listen here young lady . . .

CAROL (*suddenly turning*): Don't you come near me!

BRIGGS (*taken aback by her vehemence, he stops*): Pardon?

CAROL: I don't want you to come near me.

BRIGGS: Well in that case just get yourself moving and let's get down to the beach.

CAROL: You go. *I'm* not comin'.

BRIGGS: You what?

CAROL: Tell Mrs Kay she can go home without me. I'm stoppin' here, by the sea.
Pause.

BRIGGS: Now you just listen to me. I've had just about enough today, just about enough and I'm not putting up with a pile of silliness from the likes of you. Now come on!
He starts towards her but she moves to the very edge of the cliff.

CAROL: Try an' get me an' I'll jump over.
BRIGGS *stops in his tracks, astounded and angered.*

BRIGGS (*shouting*): Listen you stupid girl, get yourself over here this minute.
She ignores him.
I'll not tell you again!
They stare at each other. It's obvious that she will not do as he bids.
I'll give you five seconds! Just five seconds. One, two, three, four, I'm warning you! . . . Five.

CAROL: I've told y', I'm not comin' with y'. I will jump y' know. I will.

BRIGGS: Just what are you tryin' to do to me?

CAROL: I've told y', just leave me alone an' I won't jump. (*Pause.*) I wanna stay here where it's nice.

BRIGGS: Stay here? How could you stay here? What would you do eh? Where would you live?

CAROL: I'd be all right.

BRIGGS: I've told you, stop being silly.

CAROL (*turning on him*): What are you worried for eh? You

don't care do y'? Do y'?

BRIGGS: What? About you? . . . Listen, if I didn't care, why would I be up here now, trying to stop you doing something stupid?

CAROL: Because if I jumped over, you'd get into trouble when you get back to school. That's why Briggsy, so stop goin' on. You hate me.

BRIGGS: Don't be ridiculous. Just because I'm a schoolteacher it doesn't mean to say that . . .

CAROL: Don't lie, you! I know you hate me. I've seen you goin' home in your car, passin' us on the street. An' the way you look at us. You hate all the kids.

BRIGGS: What . . . why do you say that?

CAROL: Why can't I just stay out here an' live in one of them nice white houses, an' do the garden an' that?

BRIGGS: Look . . . Carol . . . You're talking as though you've given up on life. It sounds as though life for you is ending, instead of just beginning. Now why can't . . . I mean, if that's what you want . . . why can't . . . what's to stop you working hard at school from now on, getting a good job and then moving out here when you're old enough? Eh?

CAROL (*she turns and looks at him with pure contempt*): Don't be so bloody stupid.
She turns and looks out to the sea.
It's been a great day today. I loved it. I don't wanna leave here an' go home. (*Pause.*) If I stayed it wouldn't be any good though, would it? You'd send the coppers to get me, wouldn't y'?

BRIGGS: We'd have to. How would you survive out here?

CAROL: I know. (*Pause.*) I'm not goin' back though.
She kneels at the cliff edge, looks over.

BRIGGS: Carol . . . please . . .

CAROL: Sir . . . you know if you'd been my old feller . . . I would've been all right wouldn't I?
BRIGGS *slowly and cautiously creeping forward, holding out his hand.*

BRIGGS: Carol, please come away from there.
She looks down over the cliff.
Please.

CAROL: Sir . . . sir you don't half look funny y' know.

BRIGGS (*smiling*): Why?

CAROL: Sir, you should smile more often. You look great when y' smile.

BRIGGS (*holding out his hand*): Come on, Carol.

CAROL: Sir . . . what'll happen to me for doin' this?

BRIGGS: Nothing . . . I promise.

CAROL: Sir, you're promisin' now, but what about back at school?

BRIGGS: It won't even be mentioned, I promise . . .
His hand outstretched. She decides to believe him. She reaches out for his hand. As she does she slips but he manages to lunge forward and clasp her to safety. He stands with his arms wrapped around her.
The other KIDS *playing football.* REILLY *with the ball trying to get past a huge row of defenders.*

LINDA (*from the side of the game*): Go on Brian, go on, go on . . . (*As he scores.*) Yes.
REILLY *letting on to her.*

MRS KAY (*entering, shaking her head to* SUSAN): I think we better let the police know.

SUSAN: Shall I keep them playing . . . (*She sees* BRIGGS *and* CAROL *enter.*) Oh look . . . he's found her.

COLIN: I'll bet he makes a bloody meal out of this.

SUSAN: It doesn't matter. She's safe, that's the main thing.

COLIN: We'd better round them up. It'll be straight home now.
COLIN *begins to do so.*

MRS KAY (*approaching* BRIGGS *and* CAROL): Carol where were you?

CAROL: On the cliff, miss.

MRS KAY: On the . . .

BRIGGS: It's all right Mrs Kay, we've been through all that. Now. If you'll just let me deal with this.
MRS KAY *putting her arm around* CAROL.

MRS KAY: Carol! The worry you've caused. Oh . . . love . . .

BRIGGS: Come on . . . everyone on the coach.

DRIVER: Back to the school then?

BRIGGS: School? Back to school? It's still early isn't it?
Anyway – you can't come all the way to the seaside and not pay a visit to the fair.
Music intro begins.

CAROL (*rushing to the other* KIDS): We're goin' the fair,
sir's takin' us to the fair.

BRIGGS (*turning to* MRS KAY *who still can't believe her ears*):
You never know, Mrs Kay — play your cards right an' I
might take you for a ride on the waltzer!
The benches have been formed in a circle to represent a
waltzer onto which everyone piles.

ALL (*sing*): We're goin' on the waltzer
We're gonna have some fun
Gonna get dead dizzy
Gonna get well spun
Hold your belly, gasp for air
Ooh! Ooh feel the wind in your hair

Sir's on the waltzer
He's takin' us to the fair

We're goin' on the dodgems
And on the ferris wheel
Going on the ghost train
Gonna giggle and scream
Don't know who's scared the most
Digga or Reilly or the bleedin' ghost

Sir's on the dodgems
He's takin' us to the fair

We've never seen him laugh before
He's not like this in school
It must be something in the air
That makes him play the fool

Candy floss and hot dogs
Gonna get real sick
Look at old Briggsy
In a kiss-me-quick
Big dipper? Yes sir please
Hold on everybody now
Say cheese . . .

Everybody forming into a group for MRS KAY's *camera.*
Everyone holding the note on the word cheese.
In this pause the two BORED GIRLS *are apart from the rest*
of the group.

BORED 1: What d' y' think?

BORED 2: The fair?

BORED 1: Yeh

BORED 2 (*considers*): Borin'!
As everybody leaps back onto the waltzer.

ALL (*sing*): Sir's on the waltzer
He's takin' us to the fair

Repeat the middle eight.
Repeat final verse.
Big finish on last line, ending with BRIGGS *being lifted onto shoulders by a group of* KIDS *and being photographed by* MRS KAY.

BRIGGS: Last one on the coach pays the fare.
The KIDS *singing without accompaniment as they re-form the coach.*

KIDS: Everywhere we go
Everywhere we go
People wanna know
People wanna know
Who we are
Who we are
So we tell them
So we tell them
We are the Progress
The mighty mighty progress

The coach re-formed and nearly everyone on board.
RONSON *running up to the coach and* BRIGGS, *who is standing waiting for him.*

RONSON: Sir, that was great that, it was great.

BRIGGS: Come on.

RONSON: Sir, can we come again tomorrow?

BRIGGS: Oh get on the bus, Ronson.
As BRIGGS *and* RONSON *get on board, the coach pulls away with everybody singing 'Coming Round the Mountain'.*
DIGGA *and* JACKIE *are sitting together,* REILLY *is with* LINDA, *arm around her.*
BRIGGS *sitting on the back seat singing with the* KIDS.
MRS KAY *stands and takes a picture of* BRIGGS *and the* KIDS. BRIGGS *still with a cowboy hat he got at the fair.*

MRS KAY: Say cheese.

KIDS: Singin' aya aye yippee yippee aye
Singing aye aye yippe yippee aye
Singing aye aye yippee
Me mother's gone the chippy
Aye aye yippee yippy aye

The KIDS *begin to repeat the next verse but weariness and tiredness gradually overcome them and the song so that they fall asleep.*

BRIGGS *rouses himself, looks out of the window. He puts his tie back to normal, feels the cowboy hat on his head, takes it off and gently lays it on the head of sleeping* ANDREWS.

LINDA, *cradled on* REILLY's *shoulder, is softly singing to herself.*

MRS KAY *is putting completed film into a canister.*

Next to her, asleep but clutching a fairground goldfish, is CAROL.

BRIGGS *walks down the aisle, putting on his jacket as he does so.*

MRS KAY (*indicating the film*): I've got some gems of you in here. We'll have one of these put up in the staff room when they're developed.

BRIGGS: Eh? One of me? What for?

MRS KAY: Don't worry, I'm not going to let you forget the day you enjoyed yourself.

BRIGGS (*watching her put the canister into an envelope*): Look. Erm . . . why don't you let me develop those? I could do them in the lab.

MRS KAY: I don't know − using school facilities for personal gain. (*She hands over the film.*) Thank you.

BRIGGS: Have them done as soon as I can.
    He sits.

LINDA (*to* REILLY): Are y' glad y' came?

REILLY: Yeh.

LINDA: It was great, wasn't it eh?

REILLY: It'll be the last trip I go on.

LINDA: Why?

REILLY: Well I'm leavin' in the summer aren't I?

LINDA: What y' gonna do?

REILLY: Nothin' I suppose . . . (*He looks out of the window.*) It's bleedin' horrible when y' look at it isn't it?

LINDA: What?

REILLY (*nods, indicating the city*): That. Liverpool.

LINDA: Yeh.
    The coach stops.

BRIGGS: Right. Come on, everybody off.
KIDS *singing as they collect their things and gradually clear the coach.*

KIDS: We had a really great day out
We went to the beach and went daft and ran about
We went to the zoo
And the fair and castle too
And Briggsy let us sing and shout
Coming back from our day out

BRIGGS: OK. Everybody off.

KIDS: Thanks sir we had a lovely day
Thanks sir and miss, it was a cracker, Mrs Kay
The best we ever had
Even Briggsy's not so bad
Never seen him act that way
He must have had a lovely day

Climbing off the bus now
Back in Liverpool
Better get off home now for me tea
Looking at the streets, the playground and the school,
Seems a long way from the sea.

Continue to underscore.
REILLY *and* LINDA, *arms around each other, getting off the coach.*

REILLY: Night, sir. Enjoyed yourself today didn't y' sir.

BRIGGS: Pardon?

REILLY: I didn't know you was like that sir . . . all right for a laugh an' that. See y' tomorrow sir.

BRIGGS (*nods goodbye to them, suddenly calls after them*):
Oh . . . Linda.
She stops and turns.
We erm . . . we'll let the uniform go this time. But don't let me catch you dressing like that again on a school outing.
REILLY *and* LINDA *go.*
The two BORED GIRLS.

BORED 1: Wasn't that a great day?

BORED 2: It was cracker. Come on.
They run off.

MRS KAY (*having checked the coach and found nothing left behind*): That seems to be the lot. Well goodnight Ronny. Thanks. (*To* CAROL *who remains seated on the coach.*) Are you going home, Carol?

CAROL: Yes, miss. (*But she stays.*)

SUSAN (*getting off the coach, followed by* MRS KAY):
Goodnight Ronny.

MRS KAY: Well that's that. I don't know about anyone else but
I'm for a drink.

SUSAN: Oh I'll second that.

COLIN: They'll just be open.

MRS KAY (*to* BRIGGS): You going to join us?

BRIGGS: Oh . . . well actually I've . . .

SUSAN: Oh come on.

BRIGGS: No, I'd er . . . I'd better not. Thanks anyway. I've got
lots of marking to do at home. Thanks all the same.

MRS KAY: Well if we can't twist your arm . . . thanks for today.
She turns and leads the others out.
Car's over here.

SUSAN (*to* BRIGGS): Goodnight.

BRIGGS: Goodnight.
BRIGGS *stands, watching them go as we see* CAROL *and the*
DRIVER *and hear them sing.*

CAROL: Why can't it always be like that
Briggsy on the fair in a funny cowboy hat
Kneeling on the seats
Singing songs and eating sweets
And the beach so big and flat
Why can't it always be like that.

RONNY: That's the end of that one, see y' girl, take care
Better get off home now to me wife
Out tomorrow morning no idea where
It's a funny way of life

BRIGGS *has reached in his pocket for his car keys. The
envelope containing the film comes out with the keys. He
stands, looks at the envelope, opens it, takes out the canister
and looks at it. He opens the canister and takes out the film.
Suddenly deciding, he opens the film, exposing it to the light,
before stuffing it into his pocket.
He is suddenly aware of* CAROL, *stood at the foot of the
coach steps, watching him. He suddenly turns and strides
past her, without a glance. She walks off clutching her
goldfish in its plastic bag.
From offstage we hear, shouted:*

PARENT: Carol! Where the friggin' hell have you been? Just get in
this bloody house!
Blackout.

Music for the Play

WE'RE GOIN' OUT

2 KIDS

Hia Les We're Goin' Out.

+ 2 KIDS

Just For The Day, Go-in Off Somewhere Far Aw-ay.

+ MORE

Out To The Country.

Maybe To The Sea, Me Mam Says I Can Go If It's Free

ALL

The Sky Is Blue, The Sun's Gonna Shine Better Hurry Up Cos It's Near-Ly Nine

This Is A Day That's Just For Us We're Goin' Out. — On A Bus.

MRS KAY'S PROGRESS CLASS

CUE: MR BRIGGS 'THAT'S WHY THE GOVERNMENT HIRED ME'   SUNG AS ROUND

① ②

Mis-ses Kay's Progress Class We're The Ones Who Never Pass

We're Go-in Out. Off With Mis-ses Kay We're Goin' Out To-Day

BOSS OF THE BUS

CUE: DRIVER 'MISS IS NOT THE DRIVER OF THIS BUS . . . I AM!'

BOSS OF THE BUS (continued)

INSTRUCTIONS ON ENJOYMENT

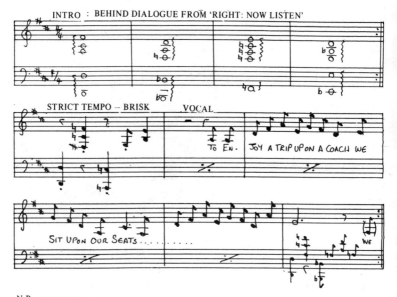

<u>N.B.</u> 'THEY'LL BE NO SHOUTING' IS DIALOGUE AND RETURNS TO STRICT TEMPO
AFTER BRIGGS 'NO SIR' FROM 'TO ENJOY THIS TREAT
DIALOGUE TO END

WE'RE OFF

LOOK AT THE DOGS

CONTINUE DIALOGUE IN RHYTHM WITH 'OUR DAY OUT' MELODY TO FADE.
*THE RIFF IN THE LEFT HAND USED AS ACCOMPANIMENT TO 'OUR DAY
OUT' REFRAIN IS ALSO USED TO ACCOMPANY 'LOOK AT THE DOGS'
AND TO REPRESENT TIME PASSING ON THE COACH. THE BORING GIRLS
CAN SPEAK THEIR VERSE OVER IT AND THE CHORDS, ALSO SHOWN,
CAN BE USED TO UNDERSCORE THE TOILET STOP.

THE MERSEY TUNNEL

*SEE NOTE

*THE BEACH SONG IS SUNG TO THE SAME MELODY AS ABOVE

STRAIGHT LINE

STRAIGHT LINE (2)

STRAIGHT LINE (3)

AL -

Come On Get In Line, Get In Line Do What You're Told For A
2(BETTER THAN A RABBLE)

Straight Line is a Wonderful Thing To Behold.

PENNY CHEWS

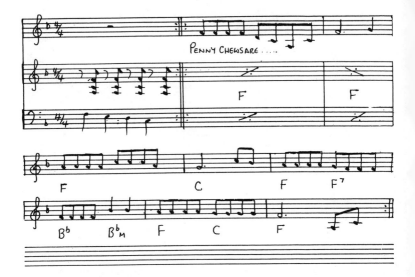

PENNY CHEWS ARE.....

F

F

F

C

F

F⁷

B♭   B♭ₘ   F   C   F

I'M IN LOVE WITH SIR

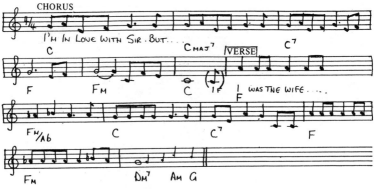

CHORUS

I'M IN LOVE WITH SIR. BUT.....

C

CMAJ⁷   [VERSE]   C⁷

F   Fₘ   C   IF I WAS THE WIFE.....

F

Fₘ/A♭   C   C⁷   F

Fₘ   Dₘ⁷   Aₘ G

N.B. SONG BEGINS AND ENDS UNACCOMPANIED

ZOO SONG

*SEE NOTES

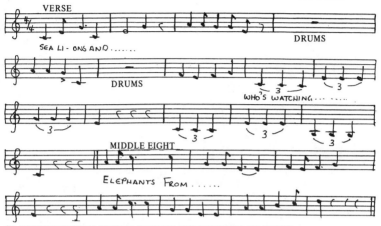

*A JUNGLE RHYTHM SHOULD PREVAIL THROUGHOUT, NO OTHER
ACCOMPANIMENT IS NECESSARY BUT COULD BE TRIED.
*THE CHANTING OF THE PHRASE 'WHO'S WATCHING WHO' AT THE
BEGINNING AND THE BORED GIRLS VERSE CAN BOTH BE SPOKEN OVER
A SUITABLE RHYTHM. THE DRUMS CAN ALSO BE USED QUIETLY BEHIND
DIALOGUE SECTIONS.

CASTLE SONG

CASTLE SONG (2)

N.B. MUSIC CONTINUES BEHIND DIALOGUE

I KNOW YOU LIKE HER

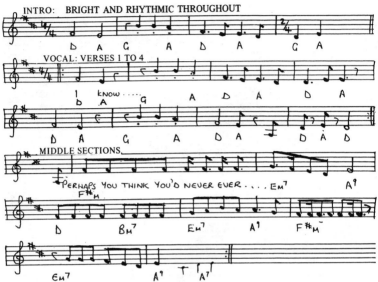

WHY CAN'T IT ALWAYS BE THIS WAY

AND: WE HAD A REALLY GREAT DAY OUT

N.B. FOR 'WE HAD A REALLY GREAT DAY OUT' USE CHORDS MORE RHYTHM –
CALLY & PLAY 3RD VERSE AS GENTLE INSTRUMENTAL BEHIND DIALOGUE UNTIL
DRIVER SINGS 'THAT'S THE END OF THAT ONE' TO TUNE OF 'SHOUTING AT THE
SEAGULLS', THEN CAROL SINGS 'WHY CAN'T IT ALWAYS BE LIKE THAT' TO VERSE
TUNE, THEN INSTRUMENTAL VERSION TO END OF PLAY. TRY TO REACH PIANO
LINE IN BAR 8 AS CAROL & BRIGGS PASS ON STAGE.

FAIRGROUND SONG

INTRO

AS MANY BARS OF STRAIGHT ROCK & ROLL
AS IT TAKES TO SET BENCHES

VERSE

F WE'RE GOING ON THE WALTZER

Bb GONNA GET ......   F

F   C or A7   Bb   C7

CHORUS

F SIR'S ON THE ... D .   G   C7   F

MIDDLE 8

Bb WE'VE NEVER SEEN HIM ......   F

MIDDLE 8

Bb   C PLAY THE FO—OL ......

EVERYWHERE WE GO

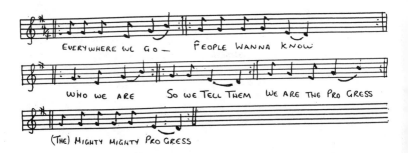

EVERYWHERE WE GO —   PEOPLE WANNA KNOW

WHO WE ARE   SO WE TELL THEM   WE ARE THE PRO GRESS

(THE) MIGHTY MIGHTY PRO GRESS

Methuen's Modern Plays

Jean Anouilh	*Antigone*
	Becket
	The Lark
	Ring Round the Moon
John Arden	*Serjeant Musgrave's Dance*
	The Workhouse Donkey
	Armstrong's Last Goodnight
	Pearl
John Arden and	*The Royal Pardon*
Margaretta D'Arcy	*The Hero Rises Up*
	The Island of the Mighty
	Vandaleur's Folly
Wolfgang Bauer	*Shakespeare the Sadist*
Rainer Werner	
Fassbinder	*Bremen Coffee*
Peter Handke	*My Foot My Tutor*
Frank Xaver Kroetz	*Stallerhof*
Brendan Behan	*The Quare Fellow*
	The Hostage
	Richard's Cork Leg
Edward Bond	*A-A-America!* and *Stone*
	Saved
	Narrow Road to the Deep North
	The Pope's Wedding
	Lear
	The Sea
	Bingo
	The Fool and *We Come to the River*
	Theatre Poems and Songs
	The Bundle
	The Woman
	The Worlds with *The Activists Papers*
	Restoration and *The Cat*
	Summer and *Fables*

Howard Brenton and David Hare	*Brassneck*
	Pravda
Mikhail Bulgakov	*The White Guard*
Caryl Churchill	*Top Girls*
	Fen and *Softcops*
Noël Coward	*Hay Fever*
Sarah Daniels	*Masterpieces*
Shelagh Delaney	*A Taste of Honey*
	The Lion in Love
David Edgar	*Destiny*
	Mary Barnes
	Maydays
Michael Frayn	*Clouds*
	Make and Break
	Noises Off
	Benefactors
Max Frisch	*The Fire Raisers*
	Andorra
	Triptych
Simon Gray	*Butley*
	Otherwise Engaged and other plays
	Dog Days
	The Rear Column and other plays
	Close of Play and Pig in a Poke
	Stage Struck
	Quartermaine's Terms
	The Common Pursuit
Peter Handke	*Offending the Audience* and *Self-Accusation*
	Kaspar
	The Ride Across Lake Constance
	They Are Dying Out
Kaufman & Hart	*Once in a Lifetime, You Can't Take It With You* and *The Man Who Came To Dinner*
Vaclav Havel	*The Memorandum*

Barrie Keeffe	*Gimme Shelter (Gem, Gotcha, Getaway)*
	Barbarians (Killing Time, Abide With Me, In the City)
	A Mad World, My Masters
Arthur Kopit	*Indians*
	Wings
John McGrath	*The Cheviot, the Stag and the Black, Black Oil*
David Mamet	*Glengarry Glen Ross*
	American Buffalo
David Mercer	*After Haggerty*
	Cousin Vladimir and *Shooting the Chandelier*
	Duck Song
	The Monster of Karlovy Vary and *Then and Now*
	No Limits To Love
Arthur Miller	*The American Clock*
	The Archbishop's Ceiling
	Two-Way Mirror
	Danger: Memory!
Percy Mtwa, Mbongeni Ngema, Barney Simon	*Woza Albert*
Peter Nichols	*Passion Play*
	Poppy
Joe Orton	*Loot*
	What the Butler Saw
	Funeral Games and *The Good and Faithful Servant*
	Entertaining Mr Sloane
	Up Against It
Louise Page	*Golden Girls*
Harold Pinter	*The Birthday Party*
	The Room and *The Dumb Waiter*
	The Caretaker
	A Slight Ache and other plays
	The Collection and *The Lover*
	The Homecoming

Best Radio Plays of 1981 (Peter Barnes: *The Jumping Mimuses of Byzantium;* Don Haworth: *Talk of Love and War;* Harold Pinter: *Family Voices;* David Pownall: *Beef;* J P Rooney: *The Dead Image;* Paul Thain: *The Biggest Sandcastle in the World*)

Best Radio Plays of 1982 (Rhys Adrian:*Watching the Plays Together;* John Arden: *The Old Man Sleeps Alone;* Harry Barton: *Hoopoe Day;* Donald Chapman: *Invisible Writing;* Tom Stoppard: *The Dog It Was That Died;* William Trevor: *Autumn Sunshine*)

Best Radio Plays of 1983 (Wally K Daly: *Time Slip;* Shirley Gee: *Never in My Lifetime;* Gerry Jones: *The Angels They Grow Lonely;* Steve May: *No Exceptions;* Martyn Read: *Scouting for Boys*)

Best Radio Plays of 1984 (Stephen Dunstone: *Who Is Sylvia?;* Don Haworth: *Daybreak;* Robert Ferguson: *Transfigured Night;* Caryl Phillips: *The Wasted Years;* Christopher Russell: *Swimmer;* Rose Tremain: *Temporary Shelter*)

Best Radio Plays of 1985 (Rhys Adrian: *Outpatient*; Barry Collins: *King Canute*; Martin Crimp: *Three Attempted Acts*; David Pownall: *Ploughboy Monday*; James Saunders: *Menocchio*; Michael Wall: *Hiroshima: The Movie*)

Methuen's Theatre Classics

Büchner	DANTON'S DEATH (*English version of James Maxwell;* *introduced by Martin Esslin*) DANTON'S DEATH (*English version by Howard Brenton*) WOYZECK (*translated by John MacKendrick;* *introduced by Michael Patterson*)
Chekhov	THE CHERRY ORCHARD THE SEAGULL THREE SISTERS (*translated and introduced by Michael* *Frayn*) UNCLE VANYA (*English version by Pam Gems; introduced* *by Edward Braun*)
Euripides	THE BACCHAE (*English version by Wole Soyinka*)
Gogol	THE GOVERNMENT INSPECTOR (*translated by Edward O. Marsh and* *Jeremy Brooks; introduced by Edward* *Braun*)
Gorky	ENEMIES THE LOWER DEPTHS (*translated by Kitty Hunter-Blair and* *Jeremy Brooks; introduced by Edward* *Braun*)
Granville Barker	THE MADRAS HOUSE (*introduced by Margery Morgan*)
Hauptmann	THE WEAVERS (*translated and introduced by Frank* *Marcus*)
Ibsen	BRAND GHOSTS PEER GYNT (*translated and introduced by Michael* *Meyer*)